girl woman wife mother

girl woman wife mother

Poems by

Talya Jankovits

© 2024 Talya Jankovits. All rights reserved.
This material may not be reproduced in any form, published,
reprinted, recorded, performed, broadcast,
rewritten or redistributed without
the explicit permission of Talya Jankovits.
All such actions are strictly prohibited by law.

Cover design by Shay Culligan
Cover image by Marleene Rubenstein
Author photo by Leah G Photography

ISBN: 978-1-63980-518-1

Kelsay Books
502 South 1040 East, A-119
American Fork, Utah 84003
Kelsaybooks.com

For the people who have made me

a girl, woman, wife, and mother—

My parents: Ima & Abba

My nucleus: Daniel

My little women: Ella, Liana, Mara, and Aliya

Acknowledgments

I am grateful to the following journals for featuring these poems, some of which may have appeared in different forms.

Anti-Heroine Chic: "When We Meet New People"
Arkana Magazine: "Guf" (Editor's Choice Award, nominated for Best of the Net)
Big City Lit: "My Father Is a Psychologist" (nominated for Pushcart Prize and Best of the Net)
Emerge Literary Journal: "Best Friends," "Song of the Submerged"
Growing Up LifeSpan Vol II: "In Highschool"
Held Magazine: "Ecdysis"
Literary Mama: "Pinata Uterus"
Rogue Agent Literary Journal: "Imposter Syndrome"
Sixfold: "Growing," "I Fall Down/I Fall Short," "Imagine a World Without Raging Hormones"
South Broadway Press: "Until Death"
Thimble Literary Magazine: "My Stomach"

I would like to extend my gratitude to poet and publisher, Karen Kelsay, and the entire team at Kelsay Books for giving such a beautiful home to house this collection of poems.

Thank you to the Antioch community, particularly the sages and my mentors, Gayle Brandeis, Alma Luz Villanueva, and Alistair McCartney. Though you mentored me in the craft of fiction, I learned skills from you that I could apply across all genres. I am a stronger writer today because of each of you.

Thank you to Rachel Kann, our bat-bayit, devoted friend, fierce poet, and gentle teacher who has always generously mentored and inspired me. I went and got my drum, Rachel.

To my siblings Yoel, Shani, Micki, and Devorah—I didn't get to choose you, but I sure am glad I got stuck with you! Thank you for always cheering on your little sister.

To my parents Ima and Abba, thank you for raising me from girl to woman. Thank you for your steadfast belief in supporting dreams. Thank you for pre-Shabbat blessings that always included wishes for my success in writing. "Abba and Ima are the very best in the whole wide world."

To my daughters Ella, Liana, Mara, and Aliya, thank you for making me a mother. It is one of the most outstanding and humbling roles I inhabit, and I pray every day that I am doing it well enough for you.

Daniel, I was a girl so that I could grow to be a woman who would become your wife and the mother to our girls—that is a destiny I would choose over and over again. I will always choose you.

I found it quite challenging when organizing these poems. Many of them felt like they belonged in multiple sections. This challenge is a theoretical extension of a daily existential one. The role of a *woman*, quite especially when that woman is a mother, is blurred and multi-encompassing. We are constantly straddling opposing and colliding identities. It is nearly impossible to fully exit one role and wholly reside in another. The variations inform one another, enrich and test our identities. These poems are fluid, they can interchange sections easily—there is much beauty in the chaos of being all things at once.

Contents

girl

Epitaph for 121 North Gardner Street	15
When Girls Who Think They Are Women	20
In High School	21
Boys	22
Best Friends	23
Tunnel Vision	26
A Jewish Girl	28

woman

Dissection	33
Imposter Syndrome	34
Write or Mom	35
Mastitis	36
My Stomach	38
Airing Out the Laundry	40
Imagine a World Without Raging Hormones	42
Song of the Submerged	43
What We Keep Inside	44

wife

Don't Stack the Plates	47
Until Death	48
Wait and Age, Please	49
I Fall Down/I Fall Short	50
Housewife	54
When We Meet New People	57

mother

Guf	61
My Father Is a Psychologist	64
When Children Die	67
Piñata Uterus	69
First Born	70
Ecdysis	71
Where Do Babies Come From	73
Mothers to Daughters to Mothers to	75
Growing	77
Hollowgram	78
ill be out in a minute	79
Just a Mother	80

girl

Epitaph for 121 North Gardner Street

I

As a child, I learn how to address an envelope. I don't like our street name, but I like our house. It is white stucco with gray shutters and grey shingles. Our house is discernable, evolving around Mother's latest creative whims. Our house has fat wide hills of grass to roll down. Sprinklers for swimsuits with straps that slip. A narrow driveway with a steep incline. Later, trellises with lopsided vines line the walkway. Mismatched ceramic pots with plants along cement steps, a shallow Tupperware of salt water for slugs that eat her garden. A slate blue, round door with a finicky lock framed by white painted metal pillars. I tell friends coming over the first time, *you can't miss it.*

II

A foyer with shiny, dark wood floors hosts the *Doodlebug* stage. The empty space fills with our dancing and singing. We perform for our parents who watch as we hook arms. Sisters vying for attention together, from each other. Father bites a bent index finger; tells us we are so *zeis*. Mother moans, exhausted, our table laden with her cooking. Kreplach. Skordalia. Moroccan fish. Pot Roast. She'd prepare feasts while glancing out an arched window at our chalk drawings. She asks for replacement legs; Bergdorf Goodman legs, she would say, not K-mart. I imagined her like a mannequin. Removable parts. Designer legs on a mother who once wore a tablecloth as an evening gown. She could wear anything and be glamorous.

III

Seated by the three-paneled, muntin dining room windows we stare at our street with a light at one end, a library at the other. We play a car game. A point for the color we choose, punch buggies double points, no punches back. Everything special happens in the dining room but family meetings take place Sunday nights around the kitchen table. Wooden chairs drag across Spanish tile; blue cushions slide over straw seats. The ribbons are always untied. Bottoms slip around as we address the agenda: a family pool or mother's garden. Mother, in a wide straw hat, measures our empty yard space next to her art studio. The garden is sectioned like a pizza pie. We all mourn the pool.

IV

Wide, flat stones sandwich the wedged dirt where sisters dig fingers for long-lost treasure but nowhere near the far back fence that separates the park because that is where our pet cemetery is. Kumquats fall like orange hail outside the bedroom no one will sleep in until they do. Big brother moves out and my hormones want space and a ceiling of plastic stars. I share the room with a fax machine until I must share with a sister again. Grandmother will sleep there. Grandfather too. But never at the same time. The room will croon Billie Holiday and World War II documentaries. The sounds rise and vibrate on my bedroom floor, mixing rock and pop. Generations collide in mechanical waves.

V

Hot water is a catcall. A wolf howl. Old pipes mean dishes and showers cannot run at the same time unless one or the other is freezing cold. And always ask if the washing machine is on before assessing if there is another earth plate shift. Walls shaking reminds us of the '94 Northridge quake; collapsed chimneys, beds wet with urine as sisters huddle in sour sheets. Neighbors share coffee in the street on portable burners. Two girls learn to sleep without a light on that January. No electricity for days. Fears are conquered but still, we will not descend the terrifying damp steps of the narrow basement nor brave the night to retrieve frozen items from the backyard art studio.

VI

Art is a living installation. We sidestep ashes in baby jars with transparent photographs of gassed children and small wooden coffins. Here, colorful backpacks are tossed amongst the Shoah pieces. Feet made of Scotch tape march across the rectangular table behind the hunched shoulders of a white sofa in front of the Chinese screen. This is where we bring esteemed guests to sit; amongst balls made of obituaries. Someone makes claim to the oil *Mayim* canvas above the still broken fireplace. No one calls dibs on the tape feet. An unused record player that once played during Purim parties where costumed guests brought homemade dishes, now collects dust in floor-to-ceiling laminate chrome wall units along with china too good to use.

VII

Bedrooms become guest rooms. New York grandchildren drag blankets across dirty kitchen floors. A grandbaby busts a forehead open during a Thanksgiving meal with twenty-plus pies eaten long into the annual Trivial Pursuit game. A new generation fears the art studio: floating pig skin dresses and the stock of expired frozen chicken and beef. Father, now Grandfather, must retrieve the frozen items along with multi-colored popsicles. In the fall, we celebrate Sukkot with around-the-world meals beneath a lattice pergola, and in the spring, matzah in Ziploc bags so guests refrain from dipping unleavened bread. We leave only to gather again next year, and the next year after that until we outgrow the roots, the house too small for all the grandchildren.

VIII

They tell us during lockdown that they are moving to live amongst Jerusalem's stones, history, and heritage. The 1926 house purchased in 1985 before gentrification, before shiny shopping centers, before Fairfax and La Brea burned in the 1992 riots, back when two tires rotated in optical illusion on the corner of Gardner Street, will sell in 2022. Boxes of our pasts arrive at our doorsteps. Rusty cookie cutters that once scraped the kitchen table of Sunday night meetings. Hundreds of loose photographs: smiling children in dated dresses, homemade birthday cakes served to classmates in the yard before it was a garden and after it was a garden, when all we ever wanted was a pool. My Little Pony dolls. Kindergarten art projects.

Stacks of camp letters asking to *get us out of here*. A 1985 Liggett's Rose Nursery catalog. Grandmother's handmade quilts, bright plastic costume bracelets that adorned Mother's long arms in the 80s. Picture books—Yellow Yellow by Frank Asch and Miss Lollipop's Lion by Judy Varga. A matzah box full of hand-sewn Barbie clothes. The Passover China. A Calico Critter playhouse. The 46" x 50" *Mayim* painting from above the still-broken fireplace. A home dismantled into brown boxes with mother's cursive spelling each of our names. Memories gifted to our porches while we are all stuck in homes of our own making. We loot, swap, save treasures from the house on 121 North Gardner Street.   I was a girl there.

When Girls Who Think They Are Women

ride in 1967 Camaros,
rusty in the joints and
old like the soul
of the boy who steers it;
the fading light of summer day
feels as long and stretched
as her legs across the dashboard.
Pacific Coast Highway wind whips
through salty hair, wilding it up
like all the worst parts of her.
Music low and slow croons,
crowded by static. Her hand ripples
like water, propelled outside
a window that is opened by a crank
handle that she twists, she turns.
So much power in just her wrist.
She stays here
where it is easier and harder
than managing female friendships—
bloody, messy and
beautiful as menstruation.

In High School

the boys said
she's crazy.
Don't trust her.
A bitch. Tease.
The girls said
they'd heard about her.
Dared one another
to prank call her.
Her boyfriend said
that her friend put the balled-up
underwear in his hand—
he never asked for it.
Her teacher, clean-shaven
cheeks plump like a baby's said
she would be famous one day.
Her classmates said
her teacher wanted to sleep with her.
The boys said
she was nothing but trouble.
Her boyfriend said
he didn't read it, but she did,
sitting in his muscle car,
her own muscles soft
as she read the letter
kept in a glove compartment,
but he said
he didn't read it.
The girls said she was pretty.
The boys said she was pretty.
But they treated her ugly
and she didn't know what
she was even though
everyone kept trying to tell her.

Boys

You both stood there
laughing.
My dress, you said,
matched the movie theater carpet.

I bought the dress for a dollar
on Melrose Avenue. I found it
buried
in a pile too loud and cheap
for anyone to reach for.
Like me.

I never wore the dress again,
not because you both laughed
but because I outgrew it
like I outgrew you.

Best Friends

If I were to write you a love poem,
I would start at the top
of your thighs. Slab of muscle,
gallop thick like ethereal equine,
a strength that could bruise me purple
with one quick flick of a limb.
So often next to you in a twin bed
I trembled in fear that your ballerina
feet might jolt, toss me over without effort.

If I were to write you a love poem,
I would start with a milkshake.
Thick, creamy, blended atop
a birch butcher block counter.
Large helpings of Breyers Vanilla Bean
and whole milk—our hands shivering
as they dropped cubes of ice. All of it
crushed, rushed together in synchrony.
With drops of blue or green food coloring,
we dyed it new, like our boring white
training bras in the bathroom sink.
We sipped it through straws, little girl cackles,
insisting it was witch's brew.
Little weirdos being a little weird.

If I were to write you a love poem,
I would start with chocolate cake.
Rich, heavy, and sweet, always from
Schwartz's Bakery on Fairfax Avenue.
Oil stains marking the pink box tied
with white string. Kosher like the pizza
from the shop with a giant round world,

a slice separated from it. I didn't know
your friends, but no one seemed to notice
the kosher cake or that you sat next to me
the whole time, held my hand
at the roller-skating party.
Both our hair long, dark, and infinite.

If I were to write you a love poem,
I would start with your bedroom window
which I could see from our dining room.
A light on did not always mean you were awake
but we had our codes,
like when you called the fax machine in my room.
Ring twice, hang up, and ring again.
I would run to answer, talk to you beneath
the ceiling of plastic stars that glowed
above me every night, each one a painful stretch
of our small girl bodies to secure them.
When stars fall, they become meteors.
Unstoppable light.

If I were to write you a love poem,
I would start with I am sorry.
Little girls say stupid things and feel
big sloppy, ugly feelings that might
wreck a friendship—wreck a person.
I should have been the first you told, but
I was one of the last and I can't even blame you.
I was angry because I didn't know.
I was angry because I made it
so that you couldn't tell me.

If I were to write you a love poem,
I would start with Facebook,
where I learned you no longer dance,
that you are handy and live with your wife
in a house in northern California with a spectacular view,
that your hair is not long anymore.
Neither is mine.
But we are still infinite.
Meteors.
Unstoppable light.

Tunnel Vision

We wore boy's wifebeaters.
Ripped them with our braced teeth.
Wide stitches held with safety pins,
our navels bared—
patches of skin peeking
through pliable metal,
inches above the jeans
that hung low on our hips.
Wisps of hair framed bronzed cheekbones.
Black tattoo chokers
stretched around our necks.

We sat in crowded hallways
where punk rockers stacked
up stairwells, blocking exits.
He sat beside me, the boy
who couldn't clot blood,
whose name rhymed with pepper,
talking of her while below us
a mosh pit swelled like angry starlings.

The headliner band was late.
The crowd; sweaty and listless.
Bodies slammed against mine.
I lost track of her, but he led me
away from harm as a song started.

and   then   it   was   boys

strumming NFG melodies on a guitar
in a bedroom where we all sat on beds.
One of them led me
upstairs to use a bathroom
where I couldn't hear guitar strings anymore.

Couldn't hear
my sister,
my friends
or his.
When I opened the door,
he was standing right there
smiling.
He must have heard the sound
of my urine splashing the toilet bowl.
What was I doing there.

I will forget this all later.
I will forget I was a girl.
I will tell her to wear a shirt
beneath the cropped sweatshirt.
I can see your belly button!
forgetting mine was once
pierced and bared and flat,
not yet stretched,
cut and sewed like the
size L boys wifebeaters
we used to wear.

I will remember the bathroom.
I will remember the boy.
It will come to me again
while I write this poem.

I will remember which boys
led me to   or   away from harm.
I'll remember boys
as I raise and tame girls
to lead their own way—always know
what they are doing there.

A Jewish Girl

Our roots are through wombs.
Genealogy traced like a child's
coloring book; easy, clear—
                         do not go out of the
                                            lines.

All six hundred and thirteen of them.

I always liked to go   out
                of the   lines.
Push boundaries.
Push buttons.
I hid jeans beneath my bed
like boys hid nude magazines.
I wore ice-cold demeanors
like girls wore red lipstick.

One single glimmer—a hair clip
amongst rows and rows
of mid-cranial ponytails
made a bearded man called Rabbi
recite my name across a high school auditorium
so that all anyone ever whispered
        was my name.
My name on notes passed beneath rows of desks.
My name across playgrounds.
My name in the back seat of a car.
My name; a four-letter word.

I chopped all my hair off in a salon
that alluded to naval dust bunnies.
She was Israeli.
She was dying.

She asked me twice
before cutting. I stepped
        out of   line.

I tried different personalities
like other kids tried different
kinds of drugs. I didn't know
who I was yet. I didn't know
the blood in my veins. I knew
only Polish accents. I knew
we kept dead relatives like
others kept photo albums.
I didn't know we also kept secrets.
I knew to be afraid when boys
called out *hiel Hitler* from passing
cars on Beverly Boulevard. I knew
the lines, and how I didn't
        fit
into
                them.

In university, they sat and talked about Jews
like I wasn't one.
How no one wanted to read another Holocaust story.
How Orthodox women only make babies.
I told the round table of writers:
I was Orthodox.
I never ate pig.
I couldn't make a baby.
They were fascinated by the pig.

We picked a nice Jewish suburb,
black hats and lace-front wigs,
kosher supermarkets with p'tcha.
When I am chasing our daughters,
holding one on a hip and another
by the hand, they tell my husband
they saw his girls with the nanny.
When someone guards my car
after a hit-and-run
in the broken gravel supermarket parking lot
she tells me:
*I thought it might have been the minivan
of one of my Jewish friends.*

No one sees I am standing in the line.
I don't even   see
                        the
     lines   anymore.

Do I look Jewish enough to you?
Do I act too Jewish for you?
Do you know that I am Jewish?
A Jewish girl.
A girl
inside
                                        outside the
                 lines.

woman

Dissection

I am wounded;
tragically distraught over
the price of Sesame Beef.
Twenty-five dollars.
I am catapulted into a panic.
Ridden into anxiety.
I see her face
as she passed me.
I am shame full.
Unsure of everything
like when
       I was young in a circle of girls
dissecting my reputation
just like the frogs in formaldehyde
that lay dead in the classroom behind us
where girls squeal as they experiment.
They poke at me—
You're not as bad as they say.

I lay awake at thirty-six,
losing sleep over the cost of velveted
strips of meat marinated in soy sauce
and wonder at the cost of inflation.
The cost of deflation.
How inside all women is still a girl.
Why didn't she just say hello?

There is no antidote for formaldehyde.

Imposter Syndrome

I wish that when you reached
for me at night you could see
how tired I am how truly tired
not just from how sore my nipples
are from nursing the baby or from
how many times I mop up spilled
orange juice but from my lack of
self-worth how my student loans
are deducted each month from the
bank account you deposit money
into or from the growing silence
in the digital abyss that swallows
my queries whole in one bite until
maybe one agent might respond
with a rejection that explains why
I will never be a writer and how
no one ever asks you if you are a
professional veterinarian but I am
always asked if I am a professional

Write or Mom

They said do it late at night.
Do it early in the morning.
They said to do it like a motherfucker.
Do it without fear.
They said to do it daily.
Do it and your time will come.
They said do it without comparing.
Do it through the rejection.
They said do it for yourself.
No one said do it as a woman.
No one said do it as a mother.
No one said you can do it all.

Mastitis

Sometimes, like maybe when
we are in the shower
and suds are cascading down my chest;
white, round, and sweet vanilla
or lemon soap I made myself
with cooking utensils that once blended round
peas and grainy apples into baby food—

                    we will remember.

The way his blue scrubs lent an authority
we both only gently challenged.
How he instructed me to remove my clothing.
How we both asked—once each—if it was
truly necessary to remove my bra and
he insisted and so I did. And you
sat there in a corner, watching my
breasts swollen with milk:
        red hot   burning   my body trembling,
chills running down my naval, my fever
so high I felt out of body,   hovering above

in full view of my nakedness   the nurse
attaching sticky EKG Leads on my bare skin.

He sat too, all of us in the room together.
        You. me. Him.
My two infected breasts
that our daughter was badly missing.
We sat.
We said nothing.
        You. me. Him.

We laugh like it was funny, but then we turn
very serious by the time the suds I made
like the daughter I made, have evaporated.
It's like we are all in the shower together.
      You. me. Him.
and I want to cover myself
even from   You.
me.   Him.

My Stomach

Wet with love,
I roll to my side.
Middle slides—
hangs from hips
like wet laundry.
Center sagging,
dragging.
Stretched taffy—
skin spread so thin
it reads like rivers of braille.
Four stories birthed,
etched into the soft center
pillow of my bellied gut.

I want to love this mound
of flesh like I love you.
Wrap my legs
around its center.
Squeeze thighs tight,
clench sheets,
scratch backs,
feel love rise up like heat,
like prayer,
like smokey incensed
salted sacrifices.

I want to feel this stomach
like I feel you
from the inside out.
Sweaty firm,

soft sweet,
vessel of muscle and magic.
Capsule of wonder and miracle
filling me with life.
Light radiating
forces of cellular
singularity.

I want to celebrate
this jelly-eyed nucleus—
pit of the fruit,
warm and quivering
fresh from delivering.
I want to bare battle wounds,
track scars
like shooting stars,
write ballads and psalms
to the glorious,
majestic mecca
of wreathed flesh
that adorns the casings
of my most powered parts.

I want to love this
mound of flesh
like I love you.

Airing Out the Laundry

When I was younger,
I once pronounced Illinois: ill-uh-noise.
Someone laughed,
said, *it's il-uh-noy.* I felt
     humiliated. As if I was standing stripped,
bared for everyone in the room to see
how I suck in my gut,
hide the valleys of stretch marks across the
round mound where my molten thighs morph
into buttocks. That everyone could see the compressions
of my girdle, the way my skin cries to escape its confines.
That everyone could see how
I fake it.

When she is young, she says:
Daddy makes money with his hands.

I wonder: what do I make with my hands?

I have made dinner.
I have made beds.
I have made mistakes.
I have made her.

I decide to let my gut loose.
Hang my faults out to dry on the clothesline.
Let the air tickle its edges as my underthings
swing in the possibilities of open air.
Let them see its tatters and loose frayed elastic.
Let them see the hidden size.
Let them mispronounce my name—
tell me it is beautiful,
tell me it is foreign,

tell me I said it wrong
and I'll show you
what I can make with my bare hands.

Imagine a World Without Raging Hormones

I'd rather the ticklish kiss
of the many-legged, wayward
black cottonwood seed.
Fibrous weaving of soft fuzz—
early summer's frosty mirage.
Dioecious, these thick lenticel
covered trunks. Female flowering,
rotund-ovate: a forest menstruation of
floating seeds aimless and certain
towards nowhere and
everywhere—
hungry to germinate,
populate the world with its
green heart-shaped leaves.

This would be preferable
to the wet kiss of a mouth,
dirtied and chapped, dehydrated
of kindness and compassion.
A chunk of earth gripped tight
in carnivorous teeth,
rabid shaking
and shaking
to tear off a greater piece
until the whole of it is

    nothing

but rot robbing the hairy fruits
of the dimorphic Balsam Poplar of

    anything

to plant its rooting hormones.

Song of the Submerged

I learned on our walk
last night that I can not
talk to you. Like cicadas
it is better to bury it all
for years and years—
emerge a battalion of crying.
Shed my exoskeleton
as I flood tree trunks, climb
up
        up
                up
to shelter in oak and maple,
hide my song—nothing
but a faint drumming
so constant you don't hear
me at all until Autumn
envelopes you, a chill
alerting you to the silence
of impending winter.

I am gone.

What We Keep Inside

our embrace
is the things of secrets.
Girlhood/womanhood secrets.
The kinds told in the dark
or in a whisper
or in a text message while splayed
for a gynecological exam or while grapefruit
margaritas sweat their glasses in a dim bar where
someone is saying, *last call*
and we believe him—grip each other
just blocks from where our children
are home with other people so
the two of us can be alone from our children
to talk about how we are never alone from our children.
We spill on each other our big
messy complicated feelings
because when we are together it
always feels like it is the last call.
By the time we walk home like lovers,
no one would suspect how moments ago,
we broke in half
and sloppily reached for each other's
pieces so that by the time we were whole
again, we couldn't tell one limb from the other's,
one problem from another's
because some things are between girls
who are women who are raising girls
to be women and it is enough
to break you if you keep it all inside.

wife

Don't Stack the Plates

Love in a marriage
is not stacking the good china.
Ignoring how he soaps only the bellies
of the Limoges dinner plates.
His joy in saving you the chore.
Going to bed together,
waking up separately
so you can re-wash each one in the morning light,
return every dish to its place in the small closet
in the dining room where you once molded
jars and jars of homemade pickled cucumbers.
Him, pulling them out again each Friday,
never the wiser,
only to clear them again reminding you
not to stack the dinner plates
that will one day shatter like
glass beneath a groom's stomping foot
on their journey overseas.
Such luck to see the jagged
shard bones of Faberge and Limoges
as if you are but a bride again,
clutching a broken plate
in a folded cloth napkin.

Until Death

One day our bodies
won't work this way—
won't fit together
coaster on tracks,
wild
ride rise fall plummet
                        into
                                    oblivion.

exhilarate
tummy turned
knotted nausea
panting
fingers clenching,
holding onto,
pushing into,
leaning back to

      There might be

bedpans,
diapers.
A neat row of teeth
soaking in solution.
Bones so arthritic
they can't bend
towards each other
    or unbend,
and still,
I will reach
for you.

Wait and Age, Please

Why would I ever
              think
you would stop
      loving
me just
                because
I carry evidence of
                living.
That you would
not want to
                kiss
every mark,
each accumulated
                inch.
With you,
I will always accept
                another
bite.

I Fall Down/I Fall Short

1.

My husband has saved two people's lives.

Lying in bed at night,
his heart pumps
a drumbeat
into the darkness,
my cheek fitting
into the crest of his chest.

He is awake.
He is not.
I talk about the usual:
The lit agent said no.
The baby has a runny nose.
The eldest finished the fourth Harry Potter.

2.

When I was pregnant
with our second,
I fell on the sidewalk
coming home from shul.
I was in four-inch heels
carrying our toddler.

He was righting
all three of us
before I even
realized
how hard I'd hit the ground.

3.

I only wear flats now.
I still don't know CPR.
I still don't know the Heimlich maneuver.
I have four daughters.

4.

There were ten of us in the sukkah.
Across the table,
the guest in the button-down shirt
started choking, gasping, grasping.
No one moved.
He coughed without sound.
He pointed to his throat.

I screamed; *Daniel*—

namesake of he who
was thrown
into the lion's den.

He ran outside,
stood behind the man,
wrapped his arms around him,
pushed into his chest.

After he saved his life,
everyone resumed eating.

5.

He cried for me,
invoking my name
like a prayer
into the answering machine.
Please, please.
Talya means *dew*,
means *morning*,
means *reliable*.

He had just saved his
eleven-year-old brother's life.
He had to perform CPR in the ICU.
He noticed the heartbeat had stopped
when no one else was there to revive it.

He called me after, called out;
Tali, Tali, please.
I wasn't there.

6.

We drive carpool.
We watch Superstore.
We argue over
who gets the better spot on the couch.

I know the shape of his jaw.
The scar on his chin.
The way his eyes water when he is tired.
I know the sound of his sleep.

The smell of his coffee
brewed minutes before I wake.
We go about our everyday.

Two people are still alive because of him.

Housewife

I do the dishes.

The headlines collect
like mismatched socks.
I read them.
Intent.
Discontent.
The world grows warmer.
Glaciers are melting faster than ice cream cones.
We stop using plastic straws.
I try putting snacks in PVA
re-usable bags that never seem to seal.
Something sticky spills once in a pink backpack
and just like that we are back to plastic bags.

I do the laundry.

I hurry daughters into my minivan
like men hurry girls into hotel rooms.
I teach them their body parts.
I teach them autonomy.
      A man raped a baby.
      And another man.
      And another baby.
      40.3 million people are enslaved in sex trafficking.
      A one-year-old baby is the youngest recorded victim.
The headlines glow at night while my girls sleep,
tired from their music lessons and
long day of private school and trips
to the pool or the ocean or the movies.

I pick up the dry-cleaning.

Another woman is killed while jogging.
She ended up in a cornfield.
Another woman is strangled
by a boyfriend on a road trip.
Their names are all over my phone.
They are all white women.
Four black women are killed daily.
I don't know any of their names.
They are not all over my phone.
I know the names of the gymnastics teacher,
and the piano teacher, and the lovely woman
who helps me clean my home.

I go to the grocery store.

At a strawberry-picking field,
families discuss apartheid, slam Jews
while my family eats our Kosher snacks
one table over and the lot of us enjoy
a summer afternoon on the land of the free
stolen from a native people whose demise would
categorically be documented today as
genocide. Apartheid. All the families
leave happy with baskets of bright red fruit.
We are all delighted with ourselves.

I do more dishes.

I have fifteen thousand miles on my car
in its third year of a lease. My entire life
fits inside a twenty-block radius.
I drive to the market.
I drive to our school.

I once drove to an empty parking lot just to
have a moment alone to cry.

I continue to read the headlines.
I continue to wash dishes.
I continue to do nothing.

A poem is a desperate attempt at activism.

When We Meet New People

When you talk past me
and ask him what he does
for a living while I juggle
babies, shifting weight
to reach down and pick up
a fallen bootie—
I busy myself with
wiping yesterday's cold
off my shoulder,
try to hold my waistband up
as a hand pulls my skirt
downwards into a
ground I never feel
firmly planted inside,
but only atop—
a loose bulb that
will never grow
because feet trample me
with endless requests for snacks.
I am holding an infant, bending
over the back of a toilet seat,
wiping a bottom by the time
he finishes telling you how
many years it takes to become
a board-certified veterinary surgeon.
We never mention
how long it took us to become
parents or earn my terminal
degree or how many years
it takes to write my novels
and how many rejections

I collect in my inbox while
my time is spent in a grocery
store and in a carpool line
or beneath a wheezing toddler
whose flesh is so hot I sweat
naked with my clothes covered
in vomit in a pile next to us.

No one ever asks me what I do.

mother

Guf

I am one body.
I am many bodies.
Bodies inside bodies.
I am my body on top
of his body,
beneath his body,
becoming
one body as we make
bodies inside my body.
I am a
breathing
heaving,
sweating body.
Breasts on a body,
sliding,
gliding
over, marked by midnight
cries that once stirred
my body. Sweet milk
staining sheets until
tight, greedy lips latched
to my body and I am
suckled like nectar
out of my body,
into baby bodies.
Now those babies
have grown into larger,
small bodies that rise
as buttery sun melts
nighttime. My body
next to his body
steadies,
readies
to be somebody,

some body
to other little
bodies
until more bodies
poke heads into
shadow cracks,
peeking,
peering,
waiting for me to emerge,
to embody
their maternal body.
I scoop reaching hands
and lead a row of bodies to
feed,
dress,
shuffle their bodies
to here and there as I wave
to other somebodies with
bodies like my body—
loosened gut and stretched
marks in lines of bodies,
forgetting already that
hours ago, I was his body.
When the home is emptied
of their young bodies
I try to remember I
wanted to be somebody.
A Somebody.
But success drifts like
a lost body and I feel
like a nobody and then
the sky is near crimson
and all the little bodies
are home again.

My body is
washing,
scrubbing,
tucking
bodies into beds.
My body is a bone
deep tired body.
It is a wandering,
wondering
wonder
of a body that
longs to be more of a
somebody but rests solid
next to his body amongst
bedrooms of their little
dreaming bodies and I know
it is enough for this body.

My Father Is a Psychologist

I

After I had a baby
I sank deep into a tub
murky with leaking milk.
Daniel had to help me in and out—
my limbs too heavy.
She, too heavy.
The small apartment fills with our weeping.
The tub drains.

II

Oh no, I said, *I can't take that medication.*
The last time, it really messed with my head.
With his eyes on the script pad, he tells me:
that was probably just postpartum depression.
She is in my arms. My feet hang over the
examination table, wax paper sticks to skin.
That word: *Just.*

III

The room went spinning one day
when I got up to go to her.
The swing propelling her wails
 back
        and
forth.
        Back
and
        forth.

A pendulum swinging.
My head swinging.
The room spinning.
I can't remember which medication, but I remember
    Swinging.
        Spinning.
    Swinging.

IV

Do you have thoughts of harming the baby?
My father asks me this.
He sits across from me in the room I grew up in.
No, I say. And I mean it.
Do you ever wish you weren't alive?
I don't want to answer this.
Instead, I assure him I will never act on it.
Later, I will hear him speaking behind a closed door.
I am a child again.
I hear those words: Post. Partum. Depression.
He doesn't say: *just.*
I never tell him thank you.

V

I tell a woman in a small office with very curly hair
that we tried a long time to get pregnant.
I tell her about plastic vaginas, needles, hormones.
I tell her about petri dishes, insemination,
surgical internships, moving to Texas,
and not knowing a soul. And having a baby.

Finally.
I tell her: I'm sad.
She tells me: *That's a lot.*
I don't go back to see her again.

VI

I leave early. I go back to Los Angeles,
to the house where my father asked me questions.
We don't like being apart from each other
but I can't snap out of it, and I blamed
Houston. The bayous, the humidity, the sudden
torrential rains. I put little white sunglasses on her
round face and we walk together on Beverly Boulevard.

My father never asks me questions again.

When Children Die

a great swelling brews.
A swarm of sadness
in the mighty belly of the sea.
It grows, expands in powerful
pounding of furious swallows
that hollow a space so wide
it could hold growing life
like a saltwater uterus.

When children die
velvet flower petals wilt
like weeping willows,
collect in mounds of faded color,
brown-edged stiff rigor mortis,
veins of waterways erupting like
wrinkles—quiver after stilled
breath scatters them across
dirt that holds tiny treasure boxes.

When children die
a torrential tantrum wakens the Sirens.
Songs sung like chiming bells,
like ringing in ears, rushing water.
A force like Phorcys fills oceans
with the darkest dark where the mothers
go to find babies turning cold
in amniotic fluid that foams like
high tide and breaks angry like grief.

When children die
we shiver,
shake chakras
bang hearts like drums,
burn essence sweet and spice.
Sound ram horns
whilst wrapped in torn shrouds.
Sit sea level low *shiva* while chanting
mourner's prayers that fall soft
like baby hair, fine and rich
as the first taste of air.

When children die,
we do not go looking
for the mothers.

Piñata Uterus

It sways before me in a weak wind.
Shredded, gutted, hanging by the thinnest string:
my piñata uterus. I look upon it the way one stumbles
upon natural disaster, fatal crash, mangled destiny.
I have been here before, bat in hand, ready to play.
Intimate with the routine, bloody mess trickling down my legs
like dripping candle wax. Hot. Burning.
Vulva vulnerable to biological fate,
biological bust. I strike hard.
Force drives it backward, away from me;
a bit falls to the floor, pooling.
I strike again, so hard a hole appears.
I want confetti, blue or pink, or daisy yellow, little ducks or
elephants with long, lacing noses. Musical rattles, lullabies,
soft, suckling lips, and milk, warm and rushing. I do not want
a bloody rain of sanitary napkins. I do not want this cramping,
bloating, ugly mâché uterus.

This round I do not fill my piñata
with needles, pills, petri dishes. Only with hope.
Hope exploding right out of the thin membrane
as it breaks. I know how it ends, the fragments:
red ribbons of uterine residue, cutting me:
bright shards of menstrual glass, scintillas of the sacred
cascading down, growing everything around me,
nothing inside me.
The shadow of a spouse stretches across my field.
Together we take a small hand each,
lead away from spliced defeat hanging from a limb.

First Born

Sometimes we joke about the time it took seven people in a sterile room to make a baby. The way my legs were splayed out like v-cut fillet and one after another a new set of eyes walked in to peer deep inside all the parts of me that wouldn't work on their own.

We imagined it as if it were a sitcom, the angle of the camera, how it would appear as if the lens were my vagina; the doctor with the German accent who said *okay, here we go.* The nurses. The gowns. The scrubs. Just eyes and eyes peering in, like the man who brought in the petri dish and never left, just stayed. They all stayed, watching her go. I stayed

on the living room sofa for days waiting for all those people's work to grow into someone. Now

she's so tall she easily rests her head on my shoulder when she cries about a best friend moving away. Her hair, soft against my chin. I smell the sweet scent of shampoo; the slight char of a hair iron and I remember all those eyes. I remember the audience. I remember how she grew first inside a dish. I wonder what eyes are watching her now. Watching her go. Watching her grow.

Ecdysis

I get down on all fours
to do cat-cow.
It hangs,
round
mound
of flesh
like a giant udder.
I want to take my fists,
pound it
like a chicken breast
until it's thin,
tenderized,
then take it out to grill
in the sun, sandwiched
between bikini
top and bottom.

I can grab it.
Fist full.
Jelly roll—
no sticky layers sweet,
just stretched,
farfetched. Regressed.
Diastasis—muscles
practicing social distancing
so, I'll never know
subtle
sexy
edges again.

Like a marsupial,
I carry
this hollowed pouch.
It swings heavy,

stores my scars,
tracks grievances,
long-lost ambitions,
herniated,
permeated,
dilated,
faded,
dated
by four birth days.

It is this very spot—
the soft center,
the spillage
of skin over elastic
waistbands, the part
of me I
suck
tuck
crank
into Spanx
where they each gravitate.
Rest their hard heads.
Place a small hand
on molting that housed
rapidly dividing cells.
A garden of tiny heartbeats.
Beautiful wasteland.

Where Do Babies Come From

Our uterus is our superpower!
She says it, legs bent,
spread,
arms extended,
like she is on the cusp
of flight.

I want her to believe this.
Believe our parts make us
supernatural.
Super.
Superior.
Not that I am afraid
to jog alone at night
because I am made up
of these woman parts
or that a man once
insisted I parade
before him so he
could assess how
much baby weight
I gained.
I want her to believe.
I don't want her to know
a boy once told me
when I was fourteen
that he wanted to fuck my brains out.
I want her to use her brains.
I don't want her to know
at a *shiva* house,
a man mourning his dead mother
recalled aloud the glimmer
of my gold bikini.

I don't want her to know
a man in a position of power
told me I was only waiting around
to make babies.
But I was waiting.
Waiting for her.
Waiting for my superpowers to work.

I watch her fly every day.

Mothers to Daughters to Mothers to

When she drove, she tapped fingers to Bach, Beethoven, the cello, a flute—it filled the red mini-van whose steering wheel once, like me, sent out whisps of smoke; an SOS. I begged for hip-hop, pop, or even the *oldies*. Water bottles, hot from the Southern California sun, rolled against my feet. Limp carrot sticks steamed in a plastic bag—bright orange and unwanted—sat rejected on the console between us. I wanted potato chips. Cookies. A soda. She offered me her half-eaten apple. I rolled my eyes, kicked a water bottle with my Doc Martens, said *Ima* under my breath like:

    A condemnation. An exasperation.
        Ima.
    A recalcitration. A manifestation.
        Ima.
    A proclamation.
        Ima.

When we ride in cars they ask for music with words. They want Watermelon Sugar. They want Trouble. They want Move It, Move It. They want snacks. Lots of snacks. More snacks but not *those* snacks. When I drive alone, I listen to jazz, creamy and smooth. I listen to the blues, Billie Holiday, Edith Piaf. I listen to nothing at all. Relishing quiet. I eat an apple, dispose of it inside an emptied Greek yogurt cup that smells the car musky. Bottles of water, half drunk, unopened, or empty, collect at the feet of the seats, roll, slide, crunch beneath tiny, dirty, sneakers. *Mommy.* It fills my minivan. *Mommy.* It fills my ears. *Mommy.* It fills me like blueshift—frequency increase, magnetic waves. They say it like:

    A salutation. A fixation.
        Mommy.
    An incantation. A declaration.
        Mommy.
    An approximation.
        Mommy. Ima. Mother.

I am   dispersed.

Someone kicks an empty water bottle with a Doc Marten.
They are *in* again.

Growing

I show her how to
grasp the handle,
glide the blade
sharp and precise
upwards on the same
leg that I once stretched
rolls of fat apart to fish
out bits of grey fuzzy
lint that she collected
there like she grew to
collect seashells from
shore sides, the Atlantic
to the Pacific. One nick—
blood balls,
slides
downwards over a
bulged ankle joint
and I think this
is how we all got
here—
from bleeding.
from wonder.

Hollowgram

Look at me, mommy.
Look
at
me.
I look.
I always look at you.
I see you balancing
on a beam, twirling
on one foot, swinging
left arm then right then left
across a roof of foot-wide spaced bars.
I see you
just as you see yourselves.
Remarkable.
Untouchable.
Invincible.
Look at me.
Look
at
mommy—
the way my form fell and spread.
The dark rings beneath my eyes.
How I calculate calories and
my worth on a scale.
The way I have chased
after dreams that drift further away
as I spend all my time looking at you.

How do you look at me?
Do you see what I see
when I look at you?
Or do you see what I see
when I look at me?

ill be out in a minute

When mothers cry
behind closed doors
or inside the cold hollow
porcelain belly of a bathtub
or on badly stained
bedroom carpet while
a television blares
hypnotic nursery rhymes
from another room—
they cry big ugly cries
that send loud shivers
down spines shaking
like tectonic plates whose
friction succumbs to stress;
reverberations felt for miles.
They cry in gulps.
Greedy and desperate
for release, hands clamping
mouths, calculated compressions
of suppression to muffle sounds,
rupture of maternal crust—
a boiling magma chamber.
A rapid river rushing wet
salty moist chunks hanging,
wiped with the back of a hand,
dragged across a wrinkled cheek
because they forgot a child's
birthday or because they forgot
the dinner long burnt in the oven or
because they forgot which trampoline
park the birthday party was at or they
forgot
                          themselves.

Just a Mother

You
    are
      such
          a
            good
                mother   what
            good
         is
      such
    a
mother
    I
 don't
    know
      how
        you
          do
            it   how
        don't
      you
    know
  how
 I
do
   what
      does
        a
         good
            mother
                do
          good
        mothers
raise their voice?

lift their shirt to see the wreckage?
set aside their dreams?
write poems about their children?
does
      a
        good
            mother
                  know
                she
            is
          a
       good
mother?
      what
         good
            is
              a
                  mother

About the Author

Talya Jankovits, a multiple Pushcart Prize and Best of the Net nominee, has been featured in numerous magazines, some of which she has received an Editor's Choice Award and first place ranking. She holds her MFA in Creative Writing from Antioch University and resides in Chicago with her husband and four daughters. *girl woman wife mother,* is her first collection of poems. To read more of her work you can visit her website or follow her on Facebook, Twitter, or Instagram @talyajankovits.

www.talyajankovits.com

www.ingramcontent.com/pod-product-compliance
Lightning Source LLC
Chambersburg PA
CBHW030911170426
43193CB00009BA/816